My State
TENNESSEE

By Christina Earley

TABLE OF CONTENTS

A Crabtree Seedlings Book

Crabtree Publishing

crabtreebooks.com

School-to-Home Support for Caregivers and Teachers

This book helps children grow by letting them practice reading. Here are a few guiding questions to help the reader build his or her comprehension skills. Possible answers appear in red.

Before Reading:

- What do I know about Tennessee?
    - *I know that Tennessee is a state.*
    - *I know that Tennessee has mountains.*

- What do I want to learn about Tennessee?
    - *I want to learn which famous people were born in Tennessee.*
    - *I want to learn what the state flag looks like.*

During Reading:

- What have I learned so far?
    - *I have learned that Nashville is the state capital of Tennessee.*
    - *I have learned that Great Smoky Mountains National Park is one of the most visited national parks in the U.S.*

- I wonder why...
    - *I wonder why the state flower is the iris.*
    - *I wonder why there is a pyramid in Memphis.*

After Reading:

- What did I learn about Tennessee?
    - *I have learned that the Lost Sea is the largest underground lake in the U.S.*
    - *I have learned that the state animal is the raccoon.*

- Read the book again and look for the glossary words.
    - *I see the word **capital** on page 6, and the word **history** on page 20. The other glossary words are found on pages 22 and 23.*

TENNESSEE

I live in Memphis. My city is known as the **birthplace** of rock 'n' roll.

The Memphis **Pyramid** is the ninth tallest pyramid in the world! It's 321 feet (98 m) tall.

Tennessee is in the southeastern United States. The **capital** is Nashville.

Fun Fact: Nashville is the largest city in Tennessee.

The state animal is the raccoon.

The iris is the state flower.

We grow a lot of
tomatoes in Tennessee.
Some of them are used
to make ketchup.

Fun Fact: Tennessee is one of the states that grows the most tomatoes in the U.S.

My state flag is red. In the middle there is a blue **emblem** with three white stars.

There are three national sports teams in Tennessee.

My family and I like to go hiking at Great Smoky Mountains National Park. Sometimes we see black bears.

Fun Fact: Great Smoky Mountains National Park is one of the most visited national parks in the U.S.

Listening to country music at the Grand Ole Opry is so much fun!

I like to ride the roller coasters with my family at Dollywood.

Singer Justin Timberlake was born in Tennessee. Olympic track and field champion Wilma Rudolph was also born in Tennessee.

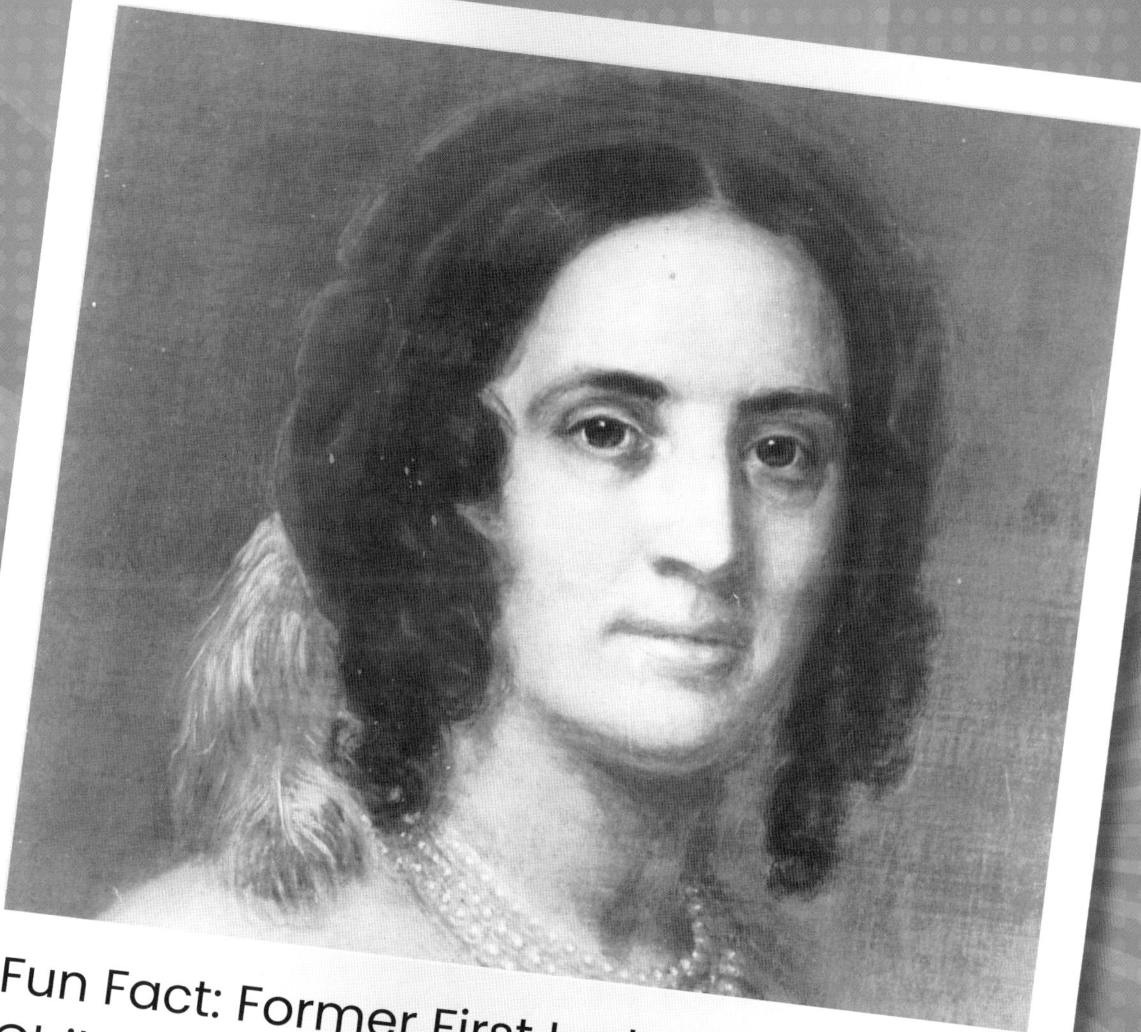

Fun Fact: Former First Lady Sarah Childress Polk was born in Murfreesboro, Tennessee.

I have fun learning about **history** at Chickamauga and Chattanooga National **Military** Park.

It is exciting to take a boat tour of the Lost Sea. It is the largest underground lake in the U.S.

Glossary

birthplace (burth-pleys): The place where something started

capital (cap-ih-tuhl): The city or town where the government of a country, state, or province is located

emblem (em-blum): A picture or design that represents an idea

history (his-tor-ee): Events that happened in the past

military (mil-i-ter-ee): Relating to soldiers or the armed forces

pyramid (pir-uh-mid): A large structure with a square base and four triangular sides that come to a point at the top

Index

About the Author

Christina Earley lives in sunny South Florida with her husband and son. She enjoys traveling around the United States and learning about different historical places. Her hobbies include hiking, yoga, and baking.

Written by: Christina Earley
Designed and Illustrated by: Bobbie Houser
Series Development: James Earley
Proofreader: Melissa Boyce
Educational Consultant: Marie Lemke M.Ed.

Photographs:
Alamy: PA Images: p. 18 right
LOC: p. 19
Newscom: MATTHEW A. SMITH/EFE: p. 13
Shutterstock: Sean Pavone: cover, p. 4, 7, 14-15, 22; William Silver: p. 3; Caron Badkin: p. 5, 23; Volina: p. 6, 22; Pratish Halady: p. 8; MOONI POONI: p. 9; lukpedclub: p. 10; Digihelion: p. 10-11; StockStudio Aerials: p. 11; railway fx: p. 12, 22; jadimages: p. 15; jejim: p. 16; Nicholas Lamontanaro: p. 17; Andre Luiz Moreira: p. 18 left; Paul Brady Photography: p. 20, 23; gracious_tiger: p. 21

Crabtree Publishing

crabtreebooks.com 800-387-7650

Printed in the U.S.A./072023/CG20230214

Published in Canada
Crabtree Publishing
616 Welland Avenue
St. Catharines, Ontario
L2M 5V6

Published in the United States
Crabtree Publishing
347 Fifth Avenue
Suite 1402-145
New York, New York, 10016

Library and Archives Canada Cataloguing in Publication
Available at Library and Archives Canada

Library of Congress Cataloging-in-Publication Data
Available at the Library of Congress

Hardcover: 978-1-0398-0536-1
Paperback: 978-1-0398-0568-2
Ebook (pdf): 978-1-0398-0632-0
Epub: 978-1-0398-0600-9